DECISIONS

Antionette Marie Courts

Copyright © 2025,

Antionette Marie Courts, all rights reserved.

No part of this publication may be reproduced, stored in a retrieval system, or transmitted in any form or by any means, electronic, mechanical, photocopying, recording

or otherwise, without prior written permission from the publisher,

Engraving Your Views. All rights reserved, including the right to reproduce this book or portions thereof in any form

ISBN HARDCOVER: 979-8-9986389-5-4

ISBN Ebook- 979-8-9986389-7-8

DEDICATION

I dedicate this book to the two greatest loves of my life.

My Mother and Grandmother, I miss you both; there will never be another like you both.

Till I see you again

TABLE OF CONTENT

DEDICATION	3
INTRODUCTION	8
CHAPTER ONE	12
I SHOULD HAVE LOVED ME FIRST	12
CHAPTER TWO	16
BROKEN PROMISES	16
CHAPTER THREE	20
NO FORGIVENESS	20
CHAPTER FOUR	24
GRANDMA'S BATTLE WITH DEMENTIA	24
CHAPTER FIVE	33
WORTHLESS CONFESSIONS	33
CHAPTER SIX	38
FRIENDS VERSES VOWS	38
CHAPTER SEVEN	44
WAS THIS HURT WORTH IT	44

CHAPTER EIGHT	49
RELAYING ON FAITH	49
CHAPTER NINE	53
TIME FOR CHANGE	53
CHAPTER TEN	57
KARMA	57
CHAPTER ELEVEN	62
A CHOICE TO BE HAPPY	62
CHAPTER TWELVE	68
SMILING FACES SOMETIMES	68
CHAPTER THIRTEEN	72
BROTHERLY LOVE, NOT	72
CHAPTER FOURTEEN	77
I CHOOSE ME	77
REFLECTIONS	81

INTRODUCTION

Many of the choices we are given determine what decisions we make, and many times our decisions can affect those close to us. God gave us freewill to make our own decisions, but that doesn't mean we can't ask God for guidance. even with that, you are still in control of the decisions you make. Throughout our lifetime on this earth, there is no doubt we will be making decisions over a hundred times a day, even if we are not given choices.

What I mean by that statement is, if your child is badly hurt, you are not going to wait for someone to give you choices of what hospitals you should go to, you are going to decide to rush your child to the nearest hospital. I had a choice to follow my dream of writing my first book or continue to do nothing and miss the opportunity to leave a legacy for my children, their children, and great-grandchildren, because faith without works is dead.

In nineteen seventy-nine, at the age of seventeen, an Army recruiter visited our high school class to discuss enlistment benefits. I was given a choice to join the military or honor my grandmother's wishes of staying home. Contrary to her wishes, I decided to enlist once I turned eighteen. This decision brought both joy and heartache. Heartache for my grandmother thinking I didn't love or respect her, but for me, it was the beginning of my independence.

My grandmother experienced disappointment because she felt I disregarded her wishes, and she felt grief due to my departure. I didn't feel like I disregarded her, but I guess I did. That was not my intention to hurt her in any way because I loved her dearly, but this was one of those decisions that affected the person I loved the most. As a child, growing up in the 60's and 70's by two strong and independent black women, there were strict rules to follow, and if you disobeyed their rules, you would get your behind beat with anything in arm's reach. Mother made all decisions for my younger brother and me until she passed, granting us little autonomy. Her guidance instilled in us the importance of education, respect, manners, and the value of honesty.

These lessons significantly shaped our behavior as we matured into adults.

(Never take for granted the wisdom of the elders)

Narcissistic Personality Disorder

According to the "Mayo Clinic Family Health Book"

(Fifth Edition)

"More common in men, the cause of narcissistic personality disorder is likely a blend of genetic and environmental factors.

Symptoms include excessive need for admiration, lack of empathy, and difficulty handling criticism and entitlement."

Chapter One

I SHOULD HAVE LOVED ME FIRST

I accepted my fiancé's third marriage proposal because he showed all the qualities of a caring partner: being courteous, saying all the right things, and treating my daughter as his own. Though I had been married twice before, I believed this time would be different because the third time is the charm, right? My family welcomed him warmly, and we celebrated holidays together. Planning our rainbow-themed wedding was exhausting, with each bridesmaid in an assorted color and matching accessories for the groomsmen. The arrangements, including the honeymoon in Jamaica, were coordinated by my fiancés best man.

The ceremony went smoothly, my grandmother attended, my brother gave me away, and our daughters were flower girls. At the reception, food came from his chef friend, and I contributed by hiring the DJ and choosing his ring. Disposable cameras at each guest table let guests capture memories; everything turned out perfect. I was offended when my husband declined intimacy on our wedding night, which I could not understand. In Nassau, we enjoyed the scenery and local cuisine, though my husband wanted to make love on the beach, which made me uncomfortable because I did not want to be on display for others to see.

We explored the island, and, despite some concerns, I felt our connection growing and wondered if this was true love. Returning home, I felt happy to be reunited with my family and ready to resume my routine, grateful for the support of my loved ones throughout this new chapter. We quickly resumed our routine with him working days and me working nights. I saw the girls off to school, made herbal tea for mom, then tried to rest before work, though mom often reflected on the past and her concerns about being a burden.

I could understand how she must be feeling, from being self-reliant to depending on someone for everything. I wanted her to feel that she was contributing to the family by taking her shopping for groceries and helping prepare meals with me. Mom was becoming weaker as the months went by, but she still wanted to do things on her own. The girls were always around, keeping an extra eye on her and letting me know if Mom needed my help. My oldest daughter was graduating from eighth grade, and I was super happy. She wore a beautiful white lace dress, and because of her long, thick hair, it didn't take much to put it into a cute bun. We attended her graduation ceremony. When her name was called to receive her diploma, I proudly shouted I love you. Afterwards we went out for a meal. Over time, my communication with my family decreased. My brother became more distant, and I saw him occasionally with his family.

I gradually realized that my husband and his sister were isolating me from my already distant family, while we only attended his relatives' gatherings. Wanting my marriage to succeed, I overlooked these changes and focused on keeping him happy and caring for our daughters. He was especially strict with our oldest daughter, but not with the other children. On weekends, my husband would stay out late playing dominoes and bid whist with friends, leaving me at home with the girls(and mom.)

He said weekends were his only chance to see his friends, so he'd go out and stay late. I never felt at ease around them; they smoked and drank, which wasn't my thing. My husband did not drink, so I wasn't concerned about drunk driving, but since I did not enjoy hanging out at other people's places, I usually would stay home. In September 1990,

I decided to tell him everything about the traumatic incident during my last training in Wisconsin, where I feared for my life after being assaulted at knifepoint.

He questioned why I did not report it, but I could not give a clear answer; my fear and disbelief that anyone would believe me were overwhelming. I didn't expect that he would later use my trauma against me. Later that month, my unit commander notified me that I was scheduled for overseas deployment with the 300th AG Postal Unit as part of the Desert Shield Conflict in Saudi Arabia, with departure planned for October 1st.

I received a general order in the mail and had to quickly prepare to leave my husband and daughters. Before departing, I arranged for my husband to adopt my oldest daughter so she could have his surname. I asked him to ensure that only family would be around our girls at home while I was away, and he agreed.

(Trust in the Lord with all your heart and soul)

Chapter Two

Broken Promises

In October 1990, I reported to my unit and was sent to Great Lakes Naval Base for deployment preparations, which included immunizations and instructions on Saudi laws, all completed in one day. My family was there to say goodbye. Our unit delivered mail and packages to the infantry by truck or helicopter. After a sixteen-hour trip, we began a six-month search for Hussein bin Laden. When January marked six months in Saudi Arabia, our orders were extended for another six months, causing me to miss important family events. Letters and care packages from home became my main comfort, and I read my daughters' notes every night before praying.

AT&T provided monthly phone call access about two miles from camp, giving us precious, timed conversations with our families. Although we longed to reassure loved ones, we were uncertain when we would return. Sometimes calls were cut off if we mentioned our location, which seemed pointless since the media at home already broadcast details of our operations before we even knew them ourselves. During my deployment, I experienced significant concern for my family back home, frequently wondering about their well-being and whether my daughters missed me as much as I missed them. I also contemplated whether my husband felt my absence. When Operation Desert Shield transitioned to Desert Storm in January 1991, intense combat erupted between infantry units and enemy forces, prompting our unit to take cover in trenches we had constructed in the sand.

The environment was hazardous; visible flames and the smell of burning oil necessitated the use of gas masks. Throughout these events, I questioned whether I would return home and looked forward to reuniting with my husband and children, wishing to reassure them of my love and ongoing thoughts during my absence. Concerns extended to my mother's health, as she had not been eating adequately before my departure. Being unable to monitor her well-being directly added to my worries.

The opportunity to contact my family by phone was a welcome relief, regardless of the challenges, including traveling at night, as hearing their voices was invaluable to me. During a conversation with my eldest daughter, I inquired if she was assisting her father with her grandmother and younger sister. She affirmed, but mentioned a woman named Michelle before my husband took over the call.

Upon questioning my husband about Michelle's identity, he initially feigned ignorance and then explained that she was someone seeking assistance in moving furniture. However, her presence around my daughters raised concerns, particularly given our prior agreement that no other woman would be around our children in my absence. This incident constituted a breach of trust, further compounded by the interruption of my conversation with my daughters, which meant I might have to wait another month before speaking with them again.

I was unable to intervene regarding his actions. He received support from his sister and niece, who assisted by caring for the girls' hair and ensuring there were groceries at home. I sent my husband $2,000 monthly for expenses, keeping just $50 for myself since I needed little in the desert. Calls were limited to less than thirty minutes so all soldiers could reach their families. Although I felt frustrated, I recognized the importance of maintaining my focus on sorting mail in challenging conditions within a hot tent in the desert. My husband wrote that he missed me, but I doubted his words.

In contrast, correspondence from the girls, including his daughter, offered genuine encouragement and lifted my spirits. On one occasion, my husband even claimed in a letter that he was unwell and requested my unit arrange for my return home. Regardless, such arrangements were not possible, nor did I wish for them. I remained committed to fulfilling my duties through to completion, understanding that this was not a situation that allowed for an early departure. My primary concern continued to be the well-being of my daughters and mother. Michelle sent a letter accusing me of being selfish for leaving him alone with our daughters, which upset me further and made me question how she even got my address; his lies were becoming obvious. I started to lose respect for him, feeling manipulated and disgusted as my anger and hurt intensified daily, and nothing he said could change that.

Chapter Three

No Forgiveness

After eight months in country, our unit was scheduled to return home in May of 1991. When the plane landed, I looked forward to seeing my daughters and reuniting with my family. I requested that a male friend stay with us for the weekend before returning to Wisconsin, and my husband agreed. My friend owned a motorcycle, and we went for a ride together. At one point, I asked my eldest daughter if she would want him to be her father; in hindsight, I recognize I should not have involved my daughter. I was not thinking straight, all I wanted to do was hurt my husband's feelings anyway I could.

In the following months, I became emotionally distant in the marriage. My husband expressed suspicions about my relationships with other men, despite having had another woman in our house during my absence. He did not acknowledge responsibility for his actions that affected our relationship. When confronted with a letter from Michelle, he initially denied knowing her, then gave varying explanations about her identity and how she obtained our address. I remained unconvinced by his responses. During this period, I dedicated time to caring for my mother and daughters and prepared to return to work. In January 1992, I discovered I was pregnant again. When I informed my husband, he responded positively. I anticipated welcoming another child and discussed the pregnancy with my daughters at an ultrasound appointment, where we learned I was expecting a boy.

During dinner, I informed our daughters that we would share the news with their dad and grandmother; however, our youngest immediately revealed that the baby had a penis. My husband responded positively, expressing his happiness about expecting a son. He selected a name for our child before his birth, choosing to name him after himself but without designating him as a junior—he appended two ones to the surname. As our family was expanding, we recognized the need to move to a larger residence, and my husband delegated the task of finding a suitable home to me.

Initially, I experienced mixed feelings regarding this responsibility, especially as I was eight months pregnant. On one hand, I appreciated his trust in my judgement; on the other, I questioned the practicality of managing such a search at this stage. Nonetheless, I proceeded as requested.

The process was challenging, largely because I no longer wished to live in an apartment regardless of its size due to concerns about shared living spaces. On August 8, 1992, while performing stretching exercises, my water broke. At first, my husband was unsure if I was serious until he observed clear evidence. He transported me to Little Company of Mary Hospital, where I delivered a healthy baby boy. Unlike previous births, our son only made a faint cry and

The doctor wanted to make sure there were no breathing issues, so the doctor admitted him to the NICU. However, I continued to breastfeed him after my discharge while he remained under medical care. Every day he was there, I would go there to breastfeed or pump my milk. Finally, the day came to bring our baby boy home and meet his sisters and great-grandmother. My husband wasted no time picking one of his female friends to be our son's Godmother. I did not agree with her being our son's Godmother because of her close ties with my husband. I know what you may be thinking, "Why would that be a problem?" My reason is that he didn't even consult with me about choosing her. Despite many warnings to leave him, I felt a strong attachment and was always there when he needed something.

While searching for a new home, I met a couple offering a short sale on their house for $13,000 — the exact amount in my trust fund. My prayers were answered when we found a house instead of another apartment. When our son was four months old, we moved into our new home, which was spacious despite having only three large bedrooms, each big enough for multiple beds and dressers. The girls shared a room with built-in dressers, eliminating the need for extra furniture. The baby would have his own room once he could sleep alone.

The house featured an open living and dining area, a large kitchen, two full bathrooms, an enclosed back porch, a finished basement, a good-sized yard, a detached garage, and was ideally situated on a dead-end street. I was satisfied with the price. The move was quick since we were coming from a one-bedroom apartment, and the new home was less than a mile away. We disregarded several items because our apartment had roaches that I did not want to bring along. Mom's Alzheimer was getting worse, and many times she would forget where she was, but I did not want to put her in a nursing home; I needed her close to me.

(love is patient, love is kind)

Chapter Four

Grandma's Battle With Dementia

One morning while preparing to take my mom to the doctor, I discovered she had left the house. Her dementia was severe; she mistook me for a kidnapper and fought back, drawing attention from a neighbor who thankfully knew our situation. I managed to calm her down and get her home, though not without scratches and bruises. After breakfast and dressing her up, we went to the clinic where she recognized her doctor, which was reassuring. I explained everything to him and showed him my injuries. The doctor advised that her condition would worsen and recommended a nursing home for her care. It was a heartbreaking decision, especially after hearing negative reports about such facilities, but I had no choice. (One afternoon she misplaced her) heart pill, and our son mistook it for candy; this led to an emergency hospital visit.

With no help and work commitments, placing her in a nursing home became necessary, even though I struggled with the decision. Although she had two biological daughters, they gave no help at all; how bad was the relationship between them? It had to be awful, that had to be the reason that they would be reluctant to help their own mother when she needed it the most; she only became my mom because my biological mom who was her youngest daughter, was killed. From the day I decided to have a nursing facility care for my mom, I felt a void that I had only felt twice before: the death of my mom and the death of my closest uncle; I lost another uncle who lived in the Virgin Islands, and I missed him too, but in a different way.

Most weekends, my husband and I would take the kids to see my mom and spend as much time as we could. On my off days, I would buy her the treats she liked, such as peppermints. I would comb her hair, which was thinning due to the wool hats she wore all the time. On a weekend visit with the kids, she did not recognize me.She thought my oldest daughter was me at that time. I knew she was getting worse; I noticed the illness of Alzheimer's and dementia had taken over her personality. I was not sure if she would ever know me again. On the way back home, I couldn't help but cry in silence. I knew nothing about this disease that was taking control of the only person who had a (close connection to my biological mom.

I would continue to visit her every chance I could. Sometimes she would remember me and sometimes she wouldn't, but if I could see and hear her voice, I would be ok. I prayed that she would not die, and I vowed to do everything I could to keep it that way. My husband would do his best to help me cope with the deterioration of my mom's health and I loved him for at least trying. During the holidays, we would pick up Mom from the nursing home to spend quality time with the family. We often had Thanksgiving with my cousins and one of mom's daughters; we had a fun time; mom was happy eating and conversing with the family and even dancing. As time went on, I saw less of my family. I would still visit mom as often as I could and instead of spending time on Thanksgiving with my family, it would be either his mom or sister's house. When I asked why we stopped having Thanksgiving with my family he would say "My mother wants to see all her kids and grandchildren for the holidays" I didn't have an issue with spending some holidays with his family. Still, we use to spend at least Thanksgiving with my family now he made a change again without consulting with me, as though I had no say so.

Our son was now one years old he had a smile like his dad and would make us laugh with his funny antics, he loved going outside to play with his sisters, He wasn't a crier, I would call him a man's baby and my husband nicknamed him "my me" because he looked like his dad and had the same name as he did. My husband used to scare me by taking our son out and ignoring my calls, playing narcissistic games. I was expected to accept it and move on, regardless of how I felt. One weekend, I decided to wash the car, so I filled a bucket with soap water and headed to the car. On the way I tripped and spilled the bucket all over me. I wasn't hurt, just embarrassed so I sat on the ground laughing at myself; then I got up to change clothes and when I got back to the car to finish the job I never started; I opened the trunk to check for a rag to wipe the car off after I washed it, what I found was his overnight bag containing clear alcohol and burnt spoon; I didn't know a lot about drugs, but I knew that should not have been there. I took it in the house and asked him why he had it, and he told me it belonged to his brother, the one who was an alcoholic, and he asked him to hold it for him. I did not want to believe my husband was using, but I knew he was lying to my face.

Several months had passed and I let go of any doubts I had about him using drugs. I guess I wanted to believe he would never do something that would jeopardize our marriage, but in the back of my mind, I knew something was not right and he seemed moody a lot. Again, I blew it off. Let me reminisce a little about the man I fell in love with, he was smooth operator he carried himself well what I mean by that is he always dressed nice and smelled so good my guy was intelligent he could take a computer apart and make it like new; he was the true definition of a self-made man, I was never sure what that meant until I met him. In the beginning of our relationship, he expressed care through actions such as placing an eight-by-ten photo of me in his car and regularly opening doors or pulling out chairs. When we walked together, he would position himself near the curb for safety. He had brown eyes and frequently smiled.

Before difficulties and changes, I felt safe with him; our marriage had positive aspects, and he was generally a responsible partner and father. Before substance use became a factor, he was modest and attentive; however, his aspirations were later impacted by drugs, certain friendships, and personal decisions. The timeline of his substance use is unclear, but in 1993, after an automobile accident resulting in significant back pain, he received treatment at the Veterans Hospital. He was prescribed Vicodin and referred to mental health services due to post-traumatic stress disorder. Initially, medication and regular mental health appointments seemed beneficial, helping him manage daily tasks and work responsibilities.

That year, we pursued approval to become foster parents by completing necessary courses for caring for children with special needs. After three months, our home passed agency inspection, and we were approved. Our first foster child was an eight-month-old girl who was placed with us after being left without a caregiver and temporarily residing in a facility for children awaiting placement.

The first time I saw her I knew right away she would be part of our family. Before she could become part of our family we had to wait and see if her mother would complete the agency's requirements within two years. That event did not occur, and her biological mother went on to have other children who were also removed from her custody. Selfishly, I felt we would be better equipped to provide her with the care and support she needed to thrive. After the two-year waiting period, we adopted her and only removed one of her middle names and changed her last name to ours. Although she was considered to have special needs, the only thing that we helped her conquer was her fear of being in the water; other than that, I didn't see why they labeled her special needs.

We briefly cared for several foster children on an emergency basis until they were placed in other homes. Our new baby girl was approximately two years younger than our son, and they interacted harmoniously. In August of nineteen ninety-nine, I received a call from the nursing home letting me know that my mother was not eating and losing weight, and they needed to know if I would consider having a feeding tube inserted that would feed her intravenously. That was a tough decision to make on the spot, and I needed time to think it over, but not too long. I reached out to her biological daughter, who was a nurse to get her advice on the matter, but she did not help me; she stated since I was making all the decisions, I should make this one too. I thought it over all day and decided to have them feed her intravenously. I would do anything to keep her alive, and if that meant feeding her through a tube, so be it. But that would not be the case. While I was on my way to visit her after surgery, I received a call requesting me to come as soon as I could because she had taken a turn for the worst.

What did they mean, the worse the surgery was supposed to make her better? I was so confused and sick to my stomach suddenly; please God, do not take the only person close to me. Did I cause her death by allowing them to place a feeding tube in her? I wonder if leaving her undisturbed might have resulted in her staying longer, as numerous questions remained unanswered. I blamed myself for her death, now it was my turn to be brave and focus because I had to be the one who would make all the calls and funeral arrangements. Grandmother had taught me to be strong when it came to situations, and this was my biggest assignment. I ensured that she was dressed all white, consistent with what our mother wore at her passing. I contacted everyone listed in her address book and selected a suitable coffin.

I arranged for the funeral to take place at her church, where we participated as children. Now, the church members would be responsible for conducting the service. After the service, it was time to place her body in the ground, which would be her temporary resting place until her spirit rested with God. Why does it take forever for them to lower the coffin? Because it seemed like it was forever. All my childhood experiences came rushing over me like a flood, and I could no longer hold back the sound of my broken heart, and my tears seemed like they would never stop. I thought I held it all together with only silent tears, I listened to all the kind words from people she crossed paths with at one time or another. I spent my entire childhood and most of my adult life, and I can honestly say I did not know half the people who were there to pay their respects and give their condolences. My grandmother/mom was a great woman, but now I had nobody to talk to, even though sometimes she would not remember who I was she would listen to me. My existence would never be the same without her. I can never forget the feeling of standing at the burial site watching as they lowered her coffin into the ground. I felt my heart sink to my stomach; I could not stop the tears from falling. (You can do all things, you are stronger than you know)

Chapter Five

Worthless Confessions

While I felt joy in caring for our new family member, the feeling of missing my mother remained constant. Soon after, I received a call from foster care agency requesting that we provide emergency foster care for a baby boy who had been removed from his mother at the hospital. Without consulting my husband, who was still at work, I agreed to accept the placement, assuming he would have no objections; however, I later discovered I was mistaken. Upon returning home, my husband expressed his displeasure with my decision to accept an emergency foster placement without prior discussion.

He indicated that he already had a son and reacted as though I had adopted the child, even though we had not yet met the baby. Nevertheless, I remained firm in my decision, particularly as he had not been actively participating in childcare responsibilities. Evening came, and there was a knock at the door. It was a case worker from the agency holding a baby boy in a hospital blanket, he only had a few bottles of formula; four to be exact, and dressed in a onesie and a pamper. The case worker gave us a brief history and said she would drop off the folder with the only information they had for him. My husband was doing his own thing, hanging out with his friends, coming in late, but I did not really care for a while because I was enjoying time spent with the baby. One evening, my husband informed me during dinner that he was using cocaine and wanted assistance.

Believing he was committed to seeking help, I asked his sister to assist him in finding a treatment center, and together we located a program for twenty-eight patients. Later I realized it was just another tactic to keep me in the marriage because he discharged himself a week after being admitted. I believe that his dependency began when his physician prescribed pain medication. Initially, he was given Vicodin for back pain; when this proved ineffective, the physician prescribed Oxycodone. I observed notable changes in his behavior, and he no longer resembled the man I met in 1984. He exhibited increased sleepiness and began to experience episodes of sleepwalking. On one occasion, I witnessed him prepare a bowl of cereal with milk in the kitchen, bring it to bed, and then fail to eat it—

each spoonful missed his mouth and spilled onto the carpet. His demeanor became markedly lethargic; he would frequently doze off mid-sentence and engage in risky behaviors such as smoking in bed. When I attempted to wake him to extinguish his cigarette, he responded by asserting, "I am still smoking." Maybe his using started way before the prescription drugs. I recall when I had a bad accident at home; I fell down the stairs and broke a disc in my lower back, and after surgery, he came to my hospital and was falling asleep instead of trying to find out how the surgery went or what he needed to do for my recovery. On the day of my release, he didn't even come to get me it was our daughter; when I needed him to pick up my pain medicine, he refused saying he was too sick and wanted me to take him to the hospital at that time I knew he was out of his mind, but he really wanted me to take care of him. When I refused and suggested he call his brother, he threw the phone at me, and I threw it back, stupid move on my part, cause just lifting my arm was extremely painful.

Although he claimed to be sick, he got out of bed and punched me in the face. I did not know what to do, so I called the police, and they called an ambulance for him because his sickness was withdrawal from the Oxycodone. Afterwards the police took photos of the red mark on my face and gave me a pamphlet on how I could file an order of protection. The police proceeded to the hospital where the ambulance had transported him; however, his brother got to him first and left the hospital with him. I did not want to keep him away from the kids, so I asked him to move out and he could have a visit with the kids. He agreed and went to stay with his sister or mother. I really did not care as long as it was not with me. That did not last long because in three months in walked into the house with his bags and said I'm back for your birthday. This was one gift I wished I could return.

I knew then I was in love with a stranger. Meanwhile, recovery from back surgery was painful, but I pushed myself to do all my therapy sessions. Learning how to climb up and down stairs was the most painful of all. The doctors told me recovery would take six months to a year, and I still would not be a hundred percent.

I started to wonder why he married me; I could have ended the marriage for several reasons, but I chose to stay for the kids. I realize keeping the kids under our toxic marriage did more harm than good. Within eight months, I was back at work, but with restrictions, even with the restrictions, it was too painful to continue to work so I resigned. My husband was still working full time, and I applied for disability, as well as filing a claim with the Veterans Administration due to Post Trauma Stress Disorder. My husband usually came home for dinner and spent time with our family, but one night he took a call at 2 a.m. and got dressed to leave.

When I asked who called, he said it was his friend, the same woman who is our son's godmother, having issues with her husband. He left without much explanation or goodbye. He returned in the morning, acting as if nothing had happened, which upset me deeply; I felt hurt and disrespected, questioning the values I'd learned from my grandmother amid our troubled relationship.

Chapter Six

FRIENDS VERSES VOWS

I began to feel depressed every day and to make matters worse, after grocery shopping, I came home to catch him brushing the same woman's hair that he left our bed to help. My first words were "What the hell is going on, without thinking twice I headed to the kitchen for a knife my mind was racing but as I was walking I was asking myself if I stabbed him, her or both are they worth me spending my life behind bars; that was a no, Instead I said you better be gone by the time I get out of this kitchen, and she was. I asked him what he was thinking, brushing another woman's hair; he had the nerve to act like that was nothing to be mad about.

I asked him what happened to the rules he set for us in our house, and he told me" That's my childhood friend, not some strange woman." I said It's still a woman and she should never be here without me, Why did you think it would be ok to be brushing her hair? What the hell is wrong with you. Did you not make vows to forsake all others, but he had an answer for everything; he told me he wasn't giving up his friends that he had before he met me. I could have ended the marriage right then and never looked back. At that point, I realized I was not the most important person in his life, or in this marriage it was he, himself, and friends, and sometimes children. My husband had broken his own rules. Those rules only applied to me, and he chose friends over marriage, along with his drug use. I began to question my worth to the point of wanting to end it all.

Hoping an unfamiliar environment would help, I looked for a place far from his pot- smoking friends, believing this would solve our problems. His comments about them kept making me angry. Though I wanted to leave the marriage, I tried to make it work and continued feeling isolated and undervalued. I found a beautiful home in the southern suburbs with a spacious kitchen and a finished basement with a bar. I know that although the environment changed, we did not.

Bathrooms, a separate dining room and sitting room, an attached two-car garage, a family room: just a fancy name for a very large living room. Everything was beautiful and the children loved the area; they had made friends instantly with the neighborhood kids. Our next-door neighbors attended the same church we began attending; my husband continued his previous employment, and I was approved for Social Security disability benefits. I was still battling with the Veterans Administration for my claim.

Everything from the outside looking in seemed like we were a happy family, but it was nothing but a facade. It had been less than a year at our new home when he told me that he quit his job. He gave me a lame excuse, he tried to make me believe that his job was downsized and outsourced, his division and offered him another position, but the pay was less than what he was originally making so he refused the position. It made no sense for him to refuse the other job; now I am stuck with all the bills.

My social security income was certainly not going to be enough to cover all the bills. I tried to get help so we could keep the house, but every turn was a dead end, and my husband was no help. The mortgage at the time was two thousand six hundred dollars. Eventually, we had to move, and our house went into foreclosure. My husband told his family that I was not paying the bill with the money he was giving me, that is why we were losing the house and had to move out. He would blame me for everything that went wrong, and afterward say he was sorry and how he loved me. Even in our new home, there was turmoil; I recall the evening I dressed sexy for him with candles the whole bit, but when he came in the bedroom, it was like he didn't even see me, then told me his brother was coming over to check the car.

I asked him if he could do that another day, his response was all I would is sex I got angry and told him, you wouldn't like it if I went to another man, would you?" I wasn't prepared for what came next. He approached me in anger and started choking me, before I realized I had blacked out, when I came to, he had left the room, and our son walked in. I'm not sure if he heard the arguing but he was mad at his dad and ran to the kitchen and brought back a knife, I quickly grabbed it from his little hands and told him it was all right, when I knew it wasn't. From that moment, I felt worthless, and nothing mattered, I wished God would take me to be with the people who loved me the most. I felt trapped in a broken marriage, and every life lesson I was taught went right out the window. The wall I had built as a child to deal with trauma was now ten feet tall. I thought the only way out of this nightmare was death, but I know it would be a sin to commit suicide; but I felt like this was hell. I had thought about suicide before and did not follow through. Even when I lost the most precious people in my life I still wanted to live. One evening, my husband went out with his friends and none of the children were home. Even though my oldest daughter had left, her relationship with her father was fractured. I contributed to the situation too, I was too absorbed in self-pity to see what was happening.

I gathered all the pills I could find and started taking them all, as I laid in our bed and started to drift off the sleep; It was true when you're about to die you can see your life fading before you, because God allowed me to look inside myself, I saw only gray and each of my organs turning from gray to black. In that moment, I wanted to live. I had a purpose, although I did not know what that purpose was. The phone by the bed began ringing. I struggled to answer it, my body had already started to shut down, but I somehow answered, and it was my oldest daughter calling just to check on me, I lied of course, and told her I was fine, just sleepy, and the conversation ended. I remember falling out of bed, asking God to help me live and not die, I was sorry that I sinned just help me. I somehow made it to the bathroom in our bedroom, crawling on my hands and knees, when I reached the shower, trying to turn the water on, but I could not stand up to reach the knobs. I began sticking my finger down my throat it seemed like nothing would work. Just as I started to give up, I started to throw up, and I could see the pills had never dissolved. I knew God had saved me that day.

Chapter Seven

Was This Hurt Worth It

Loneliness isn't just being alone, you can feel isolated even in a crowd, which is how I felt during my marriage. I lost my dignity, independence, and self-worth, and questioned why I missed the warning signs and how to regain myself. Our relationship was so toxic that we overlooked its impact on our children. Love should not be constant heartache and disappointment. I often asked if it was worth saving. Even with degrees in psychology and interdisciplinary studies, I failed to see the signs of abuse and addiction. I loved a man who once loved me, but that love became control and manipulation. While everything I did was for him and our children, lately he criticizes every action I take.

I have lost sight of myself and struggled to be the person my grandmother taught me to be. Though I know God loves me, I realized I did not love myself. Not all thirty years of marriage were bad, just the last fifteen. We had six wonderful children together. I returned to church as a Christian, not a Catholic, and was surprised when he and the kids joined me. I questioned whether this was truly an answer to my prayers or another tactic to keep me in the marriage. After the first Sunday, we attended regularly. Initially, it felt good, but soon he wanted recognition in the church. Eventually, the pastor made him a Deacon, fulfilling his desire for status. I used to criticize women for not leaving their abuser, but here I was doing the same thing at the expense of our children. There were many times when I just wanted to slit his throat, but he was the father of our children, and I never wanted them to grow up like me, without a dad, plus I truly believed he would change.

Now he was using God's word to his advantage, when I didn't agree with ideas to start a business he would quote Genesis 2:18, "this verse is the foundation for the concept of marriage as a partnership and relational support system between a man and woman" but his version was always one sided, I was the one to help him in everything he decided to do even if it agreeing was a sin.

When I corrected him, the true meaning applied to both the husband and the wife equally. He often claimed delegation was his strength; however, I grew increasingly frustrated with the inconsistency between his words and actions, a sentiment that our older children also observed. He made it clear that only God can judge him, which, of course, was true. My situation became so severe that I began seeing a psychologist regularly at the Veteran Center, thankfully at no cost. I was prescribed medication for anxiety, depression, and sleep, though in limited amounts due to a previous suicide attempt. I was diagnosed with dissociative personality disorder, which involves losing connections between thoughts and memories (mayoclinic.org). That sounded right, I wanted to detach myself from the marriage and cast out the little girl inside of me for being hopeless.

I would see other men behind his back just because I could, then turn around and tell him because of the guilt I carried: when they got too clingy, I would stop spending time with them. I had no feeling of attachment to any of the guys; I even had sex with a convicted murderer who spent only seventeen years in prison. That was a big mistake, but I did not care at the time I was reckless and wild, seeking death by stupidity. This man would follow me around secretly to see if I was seeing someone else other than him, he knew I was married and would use that against me to keep me under his control. He even showed up at my house when I would not pick up his calls. My daughter answered the door, and he gave her a large envelope. Inside it was a three-page letter about everything we had done together, but luckily I was the only one to read it. I was pissed off at what he did, I drove to the Veteran's apartment, where he resided. I saw him talking to another tenant, but I did not care and tore the envelope with the letter inside and called him a bitch, then left.

After that day, he never tried to contact me again, but my husband found out about him and never let me live it down. I was the scum of the earth in his eyes, and he let me know that daily. At one point, he told me, "If I were any other man, I would be kicking your ass." There is a saying that sticks and stones may break your bones, but words will never hurt me, but all three can damage you.

I did not care that he knew about the affair, cause when he asked me to come back home, I told him myself, so he could make a clear decision if he really wanted me home. My children would always be the reason I continued to stay and kept coming back; the only difference now was that there was no love left inside me for him, just disgust and hate. As I sat here in front of this computer, I realized there was no way I would stay for the kids when every moment of every day, I wanted to die. What if I succeeded in my sorry attempt to be free? What would have happened to my kids if he continued to use drugs? I did not really think it through; I was only thinking of myself.

Chapter Eight

Relaying On Faith

In 2013, we needed to relocate because rent payments had not been made. There was disagreement over financial management, with conflicting accounts regarding spending habits. This time, my daughter and I were searching for a new residence in July, as the landlord requested that we move out by August tenth and did not return our deposit. On August third we inquired about an apartment with three bedrooms and one bathroom, there was an unfinished basement that had a washer and dryer, and I basically begged the landlord to allow us to move in that same week, I was happy that he agreed. I was not happy that my husband caused us to move again.

I had enough of packing and moving from place to place; he would not take responsibility for his actions but would tell our children and his family I was the cause. All the years I prayed he would change, but things would go from bad to worse. I suppose God did not answer my prayers because of all the commandments I broke of Thou shalt not kill. I did not kill another person, I was just attempting to kill myself; I realize that is a cop-out, but at the time I felt there was no way to escape from this life I was living. Every morning was always the same; I would get up in time to see the girls walk to the bus stop or walk to the school bus stop with them. My husband would still be in bed; when he woke up, he would smoke a cigarette, watch television, smoke another cigarette, his attitude was shitty at best, and so was mine.

In September of twenty thirteen, I received a letter from the veteran Administration that they had approved my claim, a decision that took over ten years, but there was a catch: I would not be able to hold down gainful employment. At first, I did not want to tell my husband about the letter, especially the dollar amount I was approved for, seventy-one thousand dollars. When I told him about the letter, he started telling me what we should do with the money. He acted like he earned the right to plan how the money should be spent, but knew just what I needed to do. First, I needed to pay his mother back for the money she gave us to purchase a vehicle, but instead of handing the money directly to his mother, his sister insisted I give it to her. I kept a promise to my husband that whenever I was approved. I would buy him any vehicle he wanted, so I took him to a dealership and brought him a cream-colored Escalade SUV. I even brought my daughter a car it was used but in good condition. I gave our youngest daughter some money, who was attending Jackson State University. I even donated money to a neighbor who had just opened her own business. Since I was close to his sister at the time when she came crying to me that she needed some money, I gave willingly. For myself, I brought clothes and held on to the remaining amount.

I gave thirty-two thousand four hundred dollars in total out of the seventy-one thousand dollars awarded to me. My husband was angry when I told him I paid his mother back the money we owed her, his issue with me was that I didn't discuss with him what I was doing with the money, honestly I didn't feel like I needed to discuss anything with him; I knew if he had his way that money would of went right up his nose or worse. He told me the money should have been spent on starting a business together, but there was no way in hell that I would start anything with him, especially a whole business.

I got him to calm down by giving him a thousand dollars in cash. It did not matter that he was my husband anymore; my loving feeling for him was long gone. I was so empty inside that his harsh words became just noise. I was tired of being used for his benefit in a toxic marriage, and nothing he could do at this point would change anything. I read the definition of toxic, and we certainly fit the description. According to Webster's dictionary, toxic means "poisonous, very harmful or unpleasant in a pervasive or sinister way". That's one definition; being toxic is defined as "someone whose behavior consistently harms or undermines others, leading to an unhealthy and emotionally draining environment.

Chapter Nine

Time For Change

I felt like trauma followed me everywhere. I hoped that once I left home in a different environment that my childhood would be behind me. The military only increased my anxieties. I've learned that no matter how far I traveled my childhood trauma would never go away. Now I needed to cope with trauma on top of trauma. My marriage was another trauma of its own; my husband had changed from the loving and humble man to a controlling narcissistic hypocrite, but I still had love in my heart for him, just not the type of love that would stand the test of time. My husband had to notice I had reached my breaking point, and it wouldn't be long before I asked him for a divorce. I recalled on a Saturday morning, he decided it would be a good idea to hold a family meeting; the only problem was that it would be only his family trying to convince me that I should continue working on myself so the marriage would work, because he loved me and wanted to work on the marriage. The only issue with that was I had no more interest or energy to continue working or hoping that our marriage stood a chance or that he would stop using drugs. We tried counseling but as soon as the counselor wanted his input, it was only one-sided and he would walk out. One afternoon in twenty sixteen, while our granddaughters were at school and he was still asleep in bed, I had reached that last nerve and enough was enough of feeling depressed, physically and emotionally abused, so I made up my mind that today I choose me.

I waited until he woke up shit, showered, and shaved to tell him my decision I even made coffee, something I did almost every morning. When I told him I wanted a divorce, he looked shocked. I guess he thought I was just talking out of frustration, and he would've been partly right, but this time it was much more than that. Without skipping a beat, I asked him to move out. I had put all my dreams and hopes aside to please him. I give up time with my family to please him and his family. My dreams of starting a business would never evolve with him on drugs. I knew love shouldn't make you feel worthless and alone, what happened to the man I first met, the man who would tell me "I love you" and make me feel I was the most important person in his life. That man was long gone, and the love and admiration I once had were gone too. There were times when I wished it were possible to go back in time, the days when we treated each other with respect and love. He was my ideal man when I met him. My husband, at one time, treated me like I was the most important person in his life and that made me feel special.

I loved him and he loved me; I felt my world was complete. Karma has a way of kicking you in the ass, and maybe that's what happened to me. The man I married previously was only to please my mother, not for love; and now I'm feeling unloved. I have a new perspective on life and the importance of freedom and peace within. The day I decided to leave my marriage wasn't hasty. It took years to realize things weren't going to change for the better, in fact it took approximately thirty years to be exacted. I've learned love has many layers, but the top layer should be to love, a life lesson that would never change. I've had many years of psychotherapy, counseling, and meditation which taught me how to cope with situations that caused depression and ultimately many suicide attempts. First, I had to look at myself and search for the reasons I wanted a man in my life; maybe I was lonely or insecure both. I was searching for a better version of myself, but that didn't make sense either. In a therapy session, I had to write a list of all the things that I liked about myself and then write down things that I didn't like. That list was much longer, no surprise there.

Chapter Ten
KARMA

I was no stranger to bad decisions, and my marriage was a perfect example of that; both he and I were committing adultery when we started an affair. I was still married, living in the same space, and he was still married but living apart. Maybe if I had waited until God sent me a man, marriage would've turned out better, but on the other hand, I know women who waited for a God-fearing man and still ended up in divorce court. My life was about to learn a lesson that only real life could teach me. Once I said those words, I wanted a divorce; his whole demeanor changed from feeling hurt to anger, and lastly desperation.

When he responded, he told me he wasn't moving unless I found him somewhere else to live; did he really think that was a threat? I had been the one finding us places to live every time he caused the landlords to put us out, so finding a place for him to go was easy. There was one big issue: his credit was still too low for him to get anything in his name. I didn't let that stop me from finding a place for him to live, I had already formulated in my mind I would lease a place in my name for the first year and he would use his part of the income we shared to pay his Trent and after the lease was up he would either put it in his name or move out because I wasn't going to continue putting the lease in my name. It took less than three months when I found a place he liked with five bedrooms, two bathrooms, and a finished basement.

It was bigger and better than where I was, but that didn't bother me if he was not with me. Finally, the day came for him to move, we had already made a list of things he could have and the things that he would leave with me, but he took several things that weren't on his list. I was upset but as they said Don't sweat the small stuff, because the big reward was, he wasn't coming back. This time my life would be different after thirty years of marriage; I would have to start all over again, rebuilding my life and reclaiming my independence. I thought getting him away from me and only co-parenting would make things easy. No surprise it only made him more upset, because he couldn't have his way, he would continue to make my life miserable. He would call me to say he wasn't going to agree to a divorce. Every time I tried to have the sheriff serve him divorce papers, he would find a way to dodge them. I didn't realize at the time that continuing to be friends with his sister would be my biggest mistake. You must understand his sister and I grew close even before the marriage; we took trips together and talked about everything. I shared my darkest secrets, and she told me hers, but never thought for a minute she would play me for a fool. My husband and I even trusted her to be the power of attorney over our youngest child and our son with autism.

There were so many things I was taught as a child; like" never let your right hand know what your left hand is doing" I thought that was the stupidest thing I had ever heard but now I understood the meaning, if I didn't tell her my every move in trying to have him served and my plan to find a home of my own things might have been a smooth process. Maybe this was all in my head, but it seemed like a well-thought-out plan against me, I knew my husband was all about money and what he could get out of me. His sister on the other hand, was a heavy gambler at the casino; I went with her sometimes and played the penny slots, and she would play in the high limit room. I noticed how obsessed she was because when she ran out of money, we would go to the bank so she could withdraw money to go back to the casino. There were times she stayed playing and I would go home, and her husband would pick her up. On the morning of the twenty-fourth in October, his lease was up, and I stuck to my word and did not renew the lease for him, so he decided to move back with his mother, exactly the place he was staying when I met him.

Since I was running out of time to have him served, because the court allows you three tries to have a person served with divorce papers. On the first attempt, I hired a private process server to hand my husband divorce papers at the currency exchange on the corner of Seventy-ninth and Vincennes, where he cashed his check every month.

Surprisingly, that month he never showed up. It was strange that all the months before, he would cash his checks at the same location, but after I told his sister what my plan was, he didn't show up. I dismissed the thought that she would sabotage my plan. It had been six months since my first attempt at getting him served with no success, so I had to be a little wiser when I attempted to have him served again. My husband had been living with his mother for less than a year and wanted to leave, because he said It was too much. The issue was that he didn't know how to deal with his mother's onset of Alzheimer's and Dementia.

He would complain that she would ask him the same question repeatedly, even after he answered her every time. A year has gone by, and my husband has been asking again for my assistance with finding him an apartment. I reminded him that whatever apartment he decided to take, I wouldn't be putting it in my name. I was reluctant at first, but then I thought maybe when he had an apartment, it would be much easier to have him served divorce papers, so he asked his sister to come along for a second opinion. Finding an apartment took a while; about four months to be exact, because his credit score was below the renting requirements. When we located one that he liked, and the apartment management approved his application, it was mid-month, which worked in his favor, because that meant his first month's rent would be prorated. I was glad that it was over, so now I could plan for him to be served.

The second attempt I made was through the court, but he didn't answer his door, and the sheriff wasn't able to serve him the divorce papers. I only had one last try by the sheriff's office so I had to be smart about it that mean keeping my mouth shut and not letting his sister know.

Chapter Eleven
A Choice To Be Happy

I was feeling confident when I arrived at the sheriff's office, because this time I had a specific location, his residence, and the time I knew he would be home, and a description of the items outside his sliding glass door; this was where he had the only red top barbecue grill in that specific building. The only thing I did not like was the fact that the sheriff's office wouldn't tell you when they were attempting to serve him, the only way I could find out was to call or wait for a notification in the mail from the court. I waited two weeks after I requested the sheriff to serve him. I was thrilled to find out he had finally been served. It didn't take long before his threatening phone calls started. I was not afraid because the threats he made were nothing new from the threats he made when I asked for a divorce.

His threats would be "if I were any other man I would be beating the shit out of you." "You'll never find any man like me; I was the best thing you ever had." I took that as a good thing. On May the tenth of twenty-twenty I was given a court date: the court would be on Zoom because of

COVID. I only had to go to the courthouse to make sure I had all the paperwork needed to begin the process. This task was time-consuming and frustrating to say the least, because of the length of time we were married and there was one minor child involved, everything needed to be precise or else I would loss the little I worked for and obtained from the death of my father. Even while going through our divorce, I was looking for a home of my own to start a life without him, although I would never have been completely void of him because of our minor child.

When I told his sister I was looking for a home, she asked if she could come along and I agreed; what harm would that do I thought, because divorce proceedings had begun at least the paperwork. I was so wrong because every house the realtor took us to see was either out of the school district or missing most haves, and she would continue to tell me I should look for a place that had a mother-in-law space that if I didn't get custody of our child, she would be close, but he would have his own place. This day we were scheduled to view three homes; this time I took my son and my adopted daughter, who was turning eighteen soon. It must have been fate because the first home that day, his sister was outside talking to our daughter while me and my son did a walk through; my son walked into the kitchen before me and I could hear his excitement when he saw it, I quickly joined him and was excited too, the kitchen was custom made with marble counter tops or at least it looked marble the oven and microwave were built into the wall of the kitchen, which the room move space, the center island had a build in cook top.

I was impressed because this was a must-have on my list. There was also a finished basement with a closet, a washer and drier that was in a separate room, my son commented that he wanted this room if I decided to buy the house. After the walk- through I told the realtor this was the one. My sister-in-law was still outside when I finished, I told her and my daughter that I had decided to make an offer. The look on her face was a look of surprise and disappointment.

She commented that I hadn't even talked to her about it or even let her see inside, in my head, I was thinking What the hell? Did she think I needed to discuss with her my decides or approval; she made another statement that "when I've made up my mind to do something, I just do it" She was noticeable upset, but she was correct; I didn't need anyone's approval on of my decision, especially not hers. Let me take you back a little on March twelve in twenty-twenty, I signed for my first home that I would live in without him. I had to be wise and tactical to convince him to sign away his rights to my home, which would consist of his signing a homestead document agreeing to give up any rights to this property. When I first asked him, he was reluctant to say the least, be he agreed anyway. I've been with this man long enough to know money would be his motivator, so I offered to split whatever they gave me at closing with him, and of course, he agreed. Although he said yes, I was still nervous that his sister would talk him out of signing, but I had hopes that my offer wouldn't fail; and it was correct at the closing, he signed without a problem, and I kept my word. After closing, we drove to the currency exchange, and I cashed the check and handed him over a thousand dollars then drove him home. I was feeling victorious like I had pulled off the biggest deal of a lifetime.

When I arrived home, I called to set up the movers. Packing wouldn't take long because I had been packing for over a year, knowing this day would come to pass. It was always in my spirit that I would be moving; I just never knew when or how, so, I wanted to be ready when that time came. The day finally came for the move, and I was excited and disappointed that our marriage had come to this after being with a man half my life and loving him in every way

I knew how it failed, regardless. It was on March 13th, 2020, the same week COVID was considered a pandemic.

It seemed like the world was on pause, but I kept the pace and settled into my new home. I bought the home as is, so there were some repairs to be done, the biggest one was replacing the roof, which had a hole and raccoons living in my attic. I had to get rid of them as well that had to be paid out of pocket, because my homeowner's insurance wouldn't cover that. After the task of having wildlife control capture all the raccoons, the roofing company could begin the work of replacing the roof and gutters. thank God for homeowners' insurance. After only a week, we had unpacked and settled in, I was happy knowing that I didn't have to worry about leaving or should I say put out, because of my husband's behavior. Some days my husband and I had good conversations, and other times it would be a tug-of-war. Even though the relationship with his sister became estranged, we used to talk every day and hang out but now things were different. Maybe because I had a different mindset and didn't agree with her way of thinking anymore. I was starting to regain my independence and could see past all the bullshit. I recall the day I stopped talking to her; I had asked her for part of the money I was giving her on behalf of my youngest son, and she told me" I'll think about it," and proceeded to question me on what I needed it for. That was never a question before, and I always paid back the money I borrowed, so I was offered. I told her not to worry about it, I would just open an account for him myself and stop sending it to her. I noticed her attitude had changed since I had filed for divorce and brought a home.

Chapter Twelve
Smiling Faces Sometimes

My sister-in-law would continue to call, and I would refuse to answer; I knew if I answered the phone, I would say something I might regret, but she kept calling, and my son answered the phone, brought me the phone, and attempted to hand it to me. I told him, "I didn't want to talk to anybody," but he said it's dad's sister so I said it loud this time so she could hear my response on the other line I didn't want to talk to anybody that included her. That chapter of my life wasn't just divorcing my husband, but his family, too. I no longer allowed myself to be manipulated and made to feel guilty when I didn't do what they wanted. As soon as I realized how much of myself I had lost by being a part of his family and started to gain my independence, I was ostracized by his family and so were my children, except for one of my daughters who disowned me as her mother and sided with my husband's family. Family functions that I had once been invited to before came to an end. I realized his family was wearing masks, and they had me fooled. Once I broke ties, I could see clearly the lies, manipulations, and use of spirits under the masks. The relationship I thought I had with his sister wasn't a relationship at all. His sister had done what no other woman had the opportunity to do, and that was to gain my trust. She had a using, manipulating spirit that would do anything to get what she wanted. Now that I was in my own space, I could begin to allow God to heal the broken parts of me, especially my heart. My grandmother taught me, "men are only human with faults, so put God first and He will give me the gift of discernment". I was only a child at the time and had no idea what she was talking about". I still had a job to complete and that was divorcing my husband. I understood more than ever what my grandmother told me as a child. I picked up some lessons in my life that I could pass down to my children. This new space allowed me to discover new strengths and patience I never knew I had. My new home gave me the solace I needed to see my life from a different perspective. As a child, I did just about anything to please the people closest to me so that they could be proud of me and love me. Now, as an adult, I am doing the same thing, but the results were totally different. As a child, when I did well, my grandmother would do something special for me, nothing extravagant, but it made me feel good to know she was pleased with me. As an adult, I would often go out of my way to please everyone around me, but it was treated like that's what I was supposed to be doing anyway. This behavior was so normal to me that I never realized I was doing it. God has provided a space to mediate and reflect; it had been so long since I had the privacy to worship in my own way and discover the new me. Everything felt different; there was a calm I had never felt before. I would wake up early in the morning, make coffee, and sit back in my gazebo where the only sounds were the birds in the trees. I was pleased that one of our children was still living with me and getting ready to graduate from high school. But even though it was short-lived because she decided she didn't want to stay with me anymore, because she said I had too many rules and felt I treated her differently than her sister. I can't say she was totally wrong I was strict, so just before her graduation, she moved out to live with my husband's sister. I wasn't even welcomed to attend her graduation. I was hurt to say the least, but so be it, I had no more fights in me.

My life would never be the same, and that was not a bad thing at all, it was a great beginning. I figured this separation and divorce wouldn't be easy because there were a lot of feelings involved, like anger, betrayal, and toxic attachment. I was determined to stand my ground throughout the procedure. All I wanted in the divorce was my name back and our youngest adopted daughter to live with me; well, one out of two wasn't bad. I felt like we both won because I had to pay him child support until she reached the age of eighteen, and she was seventeen at the time of the divorce, because she decided to stay with him, and I was given permission to use my birth name.

Finally, after thirty plus years, I was free to live a new life, don't get me wrong, I still loved the man, but not like before. Like I said earlier, there were a lot of feelings involved, but when I'm done with someone, I become emotionally detached forever; something I guess I need to work on, or not.

Chapter Thirteen

Brotherly Love, Not

The year is now twenty-twenty one, my divorce is officially over, and now it was my youngest son, me, and my service dog. I was able to reconnect with my brother and spend quality time together; we even went to the movies together sometimes. There was even a time when he let me spend the night at his apartment by the lake after a vendor event that ended late, and I was too tired to drive home.

One morning, when we went for coffee, he began telling me about his living situation and how his landlord was having him take care of the building complex in exchange he would be able to rent and apartment there; yeah you read right pay rent, that didn't seem like an exchange to me, but he agreed with the deal at the time. But now he was feeling used by the landlord and he thought paying a thousand dollars a month and taking care of the property was just too much. Not thinking things through, I made a rash decision and offered my brother a place to stay at my home. At first, he was reluctant, but he decided to take me up on my offer. My only request was for him to help with the groceries and would take care of the rest; he agreed. The year is now Twenty twenty-four and my confidence is becoming stronger every day. I continued sessions with my therapist and psychologist regularly, just to keep me from falling deep in; if you know what I mean (suicide) which I had attempted many times during the marriage. There were times when he would still feel the need to disturb my peace, but I would ignore him if it had nothing to do with our child. Because he knew I would respond when it came to her, that's when he would demand I do what he wanted like the marriage wasn't over. One day he walked to the nearby emergency room and knocked on my door asking me to drive him home. I knew all he wanted was to see inside my home. Although we were divorced, I still had soul ties that would never go away. I never knew what that meant at the time, but now I know what that meant for me. According to Google "a soul tie is a strong, often spiritual or emotional, connection between two people." When it comes to spiritual and emotion, a soul tie is "those connections that can affect a person's thoughts, emotions, and spiritual well-being, sometimes influencing their energy and sense of self." I can't say I understand anything my ex-husband was going through because I never used drugs or smoked, but I did know that the man I once knew was not the man I divorced; he was long gone. Since we divorced, he has become sick a lot, and at one time, he asked me to take him to his doctor because he needed pain medication.

When his doctor refused, he became very angry. I heard the doctor telling him that he was a very sick man. The doctor never said why or what he was sick with, at least not in front of me and neither did my ex-husband. Since we weren't together, I didn't ask if he wanted me to know I figured he would tell me. In the year twenty twenty-two, our youngest daughter requested to live with me because she found out she was having a baby, and that didn't sit well with him. He did not approve her request. In fact, she called me from outside in the area where she stayed with him, and I drove to her and brought her home with me. When he found out that she was with me that really drove him off the deep end to say the least. He called the police and told them I took her, not that she called me to get her.

The police came to my house and asked if she was with me, of course I said yes, he asked me to speak with her. I called my daughter to the door where they spoke briefly, afterwards, the officer told me I was not in any trouble because she was seventeen and chose to be with me of her own free will. Of course, he wasn't happy about the situation, and he let me know it, by calling me and threatening to have me arrested by lying to me that it wasn't safe for her to be with me. I wasn't worried; I knew it was just his anger, and I was used to that. It wasn't that he would be alone because our eldest son spent a lot of time there with him too, just not permanently. There were times when he was calm and respectful, but I would still stay my distance. At one point, he asked if I wanted to take him to his storage shed so he could give me stuff that he couldn't keep anymore. I refused because there was a lot of pinned-up anger in me, and I didn't want to give him the satisfaction of doing anything he wanted me to do, so like a child, I said no and drove off. My attitude was shitty toward him; there was so much animosity in my heart, even if he was trying to do something nice, I wanted nothing to do with him.

I knew a lot of my anger was towards who he had become and the things this other person put me through. Nothing would ever be the same, I think he knew it too. There was a day he wanted to talk to me face to face, I started to refuse, but I went anyway. We sat face to face on his couch, and he asked if he could live with me; he even had tears in his eyes.

It hurt my heart to see him this way, but I needed to stand flat-footed and push my emotions aside to say no. I told him that I couldn't go backwards, and if he was still using drugs, I could never take him back, as hard as it was for him to hear he understood. I found out he had been in and out of the hospital, but nobody would tell me why, not even him. After one of his hospital stays, he told me they had to do CPR because his heart stopped. I never knew what was going on with him. I thought maybe it was the drugs he was using that caused his heart to stop, but he finally told me his kidneys were failing, and he was now on dialysis. It had gotten to the point that there was nothing that could be done; a kidney transplant was not an option.

On the afternoon of January 20th, 2023, I received the call that the man I once loved had died in Michigan and would be buried there, away from his children. Although his family didn't want us to see him at his funeral, I rented an SUV and drove our children there to have closure. I feel that chapter of my life is sealed with this book. I chose to let go and let God. Although that part of my life is sealed, it could never be erased. I made a choice a long time ago to love, cherish and honor the man I married; but the choice he made after our vows determined our future.

Chapter Fourteen
I Choose Me

Now, at the age of sixty-three, I see the world differently. I'm not that naïve woman who couldn't see the forest for the trees. Life has caused me to make choices I never thought I would need to make, for one, loving my great-granddaughter as much as I do. Don't misunderstand me. I love and adore all my grandchildren, but there's something extra special about her spirit that connects with the silent part of me. Her smiling face and witty attitude inspire me; she makes me want to live out loud.

The choices I have made in my life as an adult and the choices made for me as a child are very different, but also the same, confusing, right? Let me explain, as a child, I had no say in the choices that were made for me, but I learned valuable lessons. Even when I disobeyed the rules, I learned about the repercussions of bad decisions. The choices I have made as an adult have taught me that every choice has consequences that let me know if that choice was prosperous for our future or not, and I am not talking just about money. I made the choice to apply to the Army at the age of seventeen and joined at age eighteen. Which taught the military had stricter rules than my grandmother, but I was more prepared because of my upbringing. My choice to marry at age eighteen was also my choice, which taught me marriage is not for the faint of heart, and I shouldn't have rushed to add a man in my life. My first marriage showed me I wasn't ready or mature enough to be a wife.

I also learned what breaking someone's heart looked like because I decided to marry and then decide to dissolve the marriage. I chose to have unprotected sex while married and before our divorce was officially over. I also chose to keep the child that came out of having an adulterous affair with an older man. Both choices had lifelong effects, one more than the other, but choosing to raise my daughter without her father, was his choice, but it would still leave an imprint on her life from that choice I made.

I learned what heartache felt like and what one-sided love looked like. I learned that the words of wisdom my grandmother told me were coming to pass, and for some reason that lesson gave me strength. Her words were loud and clear in my head, "Just because you have a child doesn't mean a man will stay." And "if you give away the milk for free, he will buy the cow." It's crazy how things taught to you as a child that you didn't understand become crystal clear. Even though my choices would affect my daughter as well as myself, God gave me grace and mercy to raise my daughter on my own.

As an adult raising my child on my own, I made another rash decision to marry a man I hardly knew to appease my grandmother and give my child a two-parent home, this decision went against everything I was taught. The choice I made to marry a man I didn't trust to be around my daughter alone, not because he showed signs of mistrust, but because of what happened to me as a little girl, I would never give him that opportunity. After two years of marriage, he began having an affair, and that showed me his abusive self. In my mind, I figured this was karma for my previous actions, but I wasn't going to stand for it, especially around my daughter, so I paid for his way to New York and divorced him. After six months in nineteen eighty-four, I decided to date a married man, who was separated just thought I would mention that; I felt he was the one I would spend the rest of my life with and almost did. Throughout the marriage, we had six children in several residences, of which we were evicted from a cat and two dogs within thirty years of marriage. This marriage was nothing like the others; it caused me to rely on every lesson taught to me as a child and the life lessons I gained along the way.

In conclusion, I just want to say if I could do it all again, of course I would make better decisions; but then again, without them I would not be who I am today. So, who am I today? Confident, wiser, content, appreciative, but most of all blessed. Life has enabled me to become a mother, an Artist, an Author, a teacher, and an outlook on life that I never had before. I will continue to experience life but in a different way by learning from my mistakes and praying to make healthier decisions. My grandmother taught me how to be independent, educated, self-reliant, and never to trust in man, only Christ, but life. I asked God every day, What is my purpose? When I started loving myself and giving my pass to God, my whole life changed for the better. I can hear clearly of the work I have ahead of me. I am filled with joy, I have never experienced before. I want the same for you, but you must trust the process.

REFLECTIONS

I am excited that you chose to read my truth. I believe you want to express your truth with your story.

I'm here to tell you that if you desire it, then make it happen, step out on faith, and you'll be surprised by the blessings waiting for you.

Don't miss your opportunity to create your legacy.

Precious Watkins: Publisher, Author of Complicated Tears, Life coach, and much more Antionette Courts: Author & Artist

Website: https://www.titlesaysitall.com/productive/life-lessons

Resources

These are some resources to help Men, women, and children of sexual abuse, domestic violence shelters:

1. 24-hour hotline Freedom House 1 (800) 474-6031

   info@freedomhouseillinois.com

2. Domestic Violence Shelter- Where you or someone you know can find nearby

Domestic violence programs and shelters

DomesticShelters.org

3. Safe Haven: Provides emergency shelters for women and children

Dial 211 to find emergency housing

Visit http://dhs.illinois.gov/helpishere and select shelter

Or call: 1 (833)-2-FIND-HELP OR TEXT THE WORD SHELTER TO 552020

4. WINGS program/Domestic violence service provider

24 Hour Hotline 1 (847) 221-5680

1 (847) 519-7820

One of the largest domestic violence service providers in Illinois,

WINGS program provides housing & integrated services to adults and children escaping from domestic violence and abuse.

(Don't wait, tomorrow may be too late)

Antionette M. Courts two time published Author of Life lessons and Decisions. With her Companion Service dog Maui. As well as an Abstract artist.

Born and raised on the Westside of Chicago, Illinois in 1962,

14-year veteran of the United States Army, Mother of six children, eleven grand children and Great Grandmother.

Antionette received her Associate Degree in Art and Sciences from Oliver Harvey Community College with a Honors in African American studies. Bachelor's degree in interdisciplinary studies from Governor's State.

Antionette has never backed down from a challenge, and it shows in her dedication to accomplishing her dreams.

www.ingramcontent.com/pod-product-compliance
Lightning Source LLC
Chambersburg PA
CBHW040234110526
44582CB00002B/54